Women Building Wealth

Habits for financial wellness

Bahiyah Shabazz

Bahiyah Shabazz

PUBLISHED BY
Bahiyah Shabazz

"Women Building Wealth" is not a "get rich quick" book. It is a book of resources and advice on improving various areas of financial distress.

Women building wealth: Habits for financial wellness / Bahiyah Shabazz

ISBN-13:978-1507682203
ISBN-10:1507682204
BISAC: Business & Economics/ Women in Business

Edited by: Lisa DeNeal

Bahiyah Shabazz

A special thanks to my wonderful, supportive family. You truly inspire me to be the best person ever!

I also want to thank each woman who disproves the myth that women cannot have it all.

Table of Contents

****

Introduction

****

"A man is not a good physician if he's never been sick." ~ Arab Proverb

There are multiple books about managing your personal finances. Some equate with your concerns, while others just do not add up.

I wrote this book to not only familiarize you with key points on improving your personal finances, Women Building Wealth will give you the necessary tools needed to live a life of wealth.

The time has come for you to create a legacy, contribute towards the well-being of self, family and able to make prudent decisions in life.

"Are you completely happy with your life?" This is a question most people take for granted. Before you answer I want you to consider your family, place of employment, and finances. If you can honestly say "No" to any of these then you are in the right place.

Write down your obstacles then revisit upon completion of reading for a solution.

Are you ready for empowerment? Then let us take the steps, together!

Over the years, I have come across individuals, couples and entrepreneurs who were interested in getting out of debt and controlling their finances. As I have grown in the business, I have learned that there are many adequate blueprints for you to follow. However, a blueprint does not make a difference if you are not willing to change your behavior.

Behavior is a habit that is conditioned in your mind. It is formed from what you see from self, in others, and the experiences you have collected throughout the years. Your habits are formed from your background, culture, and socioeconomic class. At times it is difficult to change because you've engaged in these actions for years.

I am sure many of you have participated in a daily routine only to find yourself wondering, how did I finish the project without realizing I was demonstrating habits that would lead to bad financial decisions?

In order to achieve financial wellness, you must have a blueprint. I can provide you with a blueprint, but it is up to you to change your behavior. A successful event is when you enter a situation, address your needs, and walk away satisfied.

I once attended a workshop that had several sessions. I joined a married couple at one table and was enlighten by their engaged conversation with each other.

During one of our breakout sessions, the wife leaned over and asked about my line of business. I informed her that I was in the business of helping others reach their goals by holding them accountable while improving both their self-worth and net worth. "Interesting!" she said. We went on to discuss everything from the books I have written to her becoming a businessperson.

Her husband was fascinated about the approach I take with my clients. He revealed that he is a smoker and tried to stop smoking for years because it is affecting his health and their money. Each time he would quit, it was more successful, and therefore, he would eventually stop smoking. However, one of the drawbacks for his lack of success was the habit of smoking.

Each time he would "quit" smoking, the smell of cigarette smoke disgusted him. However, he could not train himself to end his habit. He tried everything to stop from sticks of gum to snack packs of candy bars. No success!

The husband received the blueprint from his doctor to stop smoking. He engaged in hypnosis, pills, and patches. Still there was no success. I eventually learned that his father and grandfather also smoked. It was a learned habit, and it was conditioned in his psyche after watching the men in his life engage in this particular habit.

The husband had to learn to change his habits. He had the desire to stop smoking, but was unsuccessful in completing the task.

We all have vices; it is up to you to point out what you must adjust. Whether it is smoking, shopping, eating, spending, or neglect there are things you can work toward improving so that you are content. Changing your habits begins with being honest about where you are in life. The point is that you must address your habits before you can begin to see the light of success. The goal is to work on you, and then the problem will resolve itself.

His wife rejoined the conversation, saying that she would not know what to do if she lost her husband. So many women can relate. Too often women spend their lives taking care of a spouse and children. They look for someone else to take care of them instead of creating a life full of wealth for themselves.

Ladies it is possible to have it all, but you must learn to put your needs first.

Do not get me wrong, not everyone can be rich. But anyone can live a life filled with wealth through wholeheartedly encouraging activities that leads to happiness. Find what makes you happy. Wouldn't it be great to live a free life? Free to make your own decisions. Free of expectations from others. Free of debt. Free to live a healthy lifestyle. Free to be an owner. In order to be happy you must strive to have a wealthy life.

Women Building Wealth contains

examples, as well as good habits that encourage you to live a fulfilling lifestyle.

In regards to finances, you are taught at an early age how to manage your money. You either notice your parents' budgeting, mismanaging, planning, or do not.

Women Building Wealth is designed for women who want to succeed and build a legacy. Women are influential in household spending, reducing debt, and supporting others. Yet they are not confident in maintaining their own worthwhile existence.

There will be many reasons that surface as to why you should not continue, but your goal is to overcome obstacles and learn to defeat the fear that consumes you from being successful.

In addition to reading *Women*

Building Wealth, I strongly suggest that you keep a journal and document your thoughts, emotions, goals, obstacles, and plan of action.

If you are consistent in writing, you will soon notice a change in yourself. A change as you see what is holding you back from wholeheartedly engaging activity leading to happiness (wealth).

****

Acceptance

****

"When your self-worth goes up, your net worth goes up with it." ~ Marc Victor Hansen

Growing up, I witnessed my mother work extremely hard to provide for our family. Yes, my dad was in the home and he too worked for a salary. I am not taking away from what my father contributed or the role he played as head of the household, but there is something about a woman who is able to be mutually supportive. She was able to contribute toward the finances by bringing home an income, make dinner, and be the person we went to for assistance with school assignments, and dilemma. My mother also made sure she kept something for herself in case of a rainy day. The household dynamics lasted until my parents decided to call it quits due to personal reasons. After the divorce, my mother became the sole provider who needed us to live a frugal lifestyle in order to make ends meet.

In my eyes we never went without. We may not have had pancakes, omelets, hash browns, and freshly squeezed orange juice for breakfast, but my mother made sure that we were never hungry. I did not realize that we lived a meager lifestyle because we were rich in family values. We were thrifty, but we also had vacations and lots of family time.

On weekends, we patronized flea markets, discount stores, and yard sales. Since we saved money through bargain shopping, we were able to take road trips during the summer.

That was the life!

We never discussed money during family time. "Because I said so" was an automatic answer from our parents.

In addition to shopping at the flea market, we also visited stores that were not so popular amongst the children at school. There was a store that we frequented, and it still exists in our old neighborhood. Imagine a store where there were no brand labels on clothing, shoes were made out of cloth with little padding, and jeans had sewn in knee pads. You could spot an item from that store a block away.

Every class had someone that others liked to taunt. I was that someone. It was amazing that I had buddies. Buddies were an inexpesive pair of shoes, not personal friends.

When I became an adult, I had no reason to say my parents' phrase. There was not a reason…I did not know how to manage money.

When I got my first job, I was on cloud 9 maybe even on cloud 10. My entire paycheck went toward whatever I wanted. From that day on, I controlled my own money and my parents did not have to buy anything for me. I lived that way throughout high school and into college. That was when I declared financial independence. At least I thought that I was financially independent. Who knew the decisions that were made then would follow me for years to come?

My financial independence was short-lived when I received my first, second,

third, fourth, fifth, and sixth credit card. Can
you believe that was all in one semester of
college? I was convinced to complete credit
card applications in exchange for t-shirts and
totes. The reality was that it would have
been cheaper just paying cash for the items.
Instead I used each credit card towards
purchases that I cannot even remember
today, that cost me thousands in interests
just to say, *'charge it'*. If I could remember
one thing it was that I looked good and no
one could tell me otherwise.

I was fortunate, or not, to work and
earn a living while attending college. I had
the opportunity to invest in a 401K and save.
I wished my adult self was able to write a
letter to my younger self to ignite the
financial prudence needed to become a
millionaire. Since that was not going to

happen I continued to spend like there was no tomorrow and I never did contribute towards retirement like I was encouraged by older colleagues. Why? As most young adults think, I had time to save for retirement. However, I did contribute over $10,000 to a 401k only to cash out later. What made matters worse was that one of the jobs I landed was in women's retail. I would unpack boxes, put my size to the side, and spend most of my paycheck before receiving it.

I used clothing to define who I was and what I wanted others to see. I presented a façade. I was able to afford more than the off-brand clothes I wore during my youth. My acceptance came with the opinion of others, not myself. The need to actually be accepted by others caused a huge financial hole that I jumped into and buried myself alive. I essentially was suffocating from plastic credit cards. The same cards that I received in college were accumulating out of control from interest rates and negative hits on my credit score. The only report that I knew and had any importance was my report card. If I had to grade myself on money management, it would have been an 'F'.

It was not until my early thirties, while working in Corporate America that I began to realize I was more than my clothing, vehicle, home, bonus checks, and the company I kept. To be honest, although I earned a great income, I was actually poor middle class. To make matters worse, I did not have much money in a savings account. I barely scratched the surface with a retirement account, and I lived paycheck to paycheck due to expenses. But I looked good! In reality, I was worth more dead than alive. Thank GOD for life insurance.

On a humbling day, I looked at myself and realized that I was a superficial person who was not able to leave a legacy worth remembering. At my demise no one would remember what I wore, the vehicles I drove, the dinners I splurged on, or the vacations I took. I did not practice unconditional love, self education and wealth building. I was not doing justice as a woman. I was not empowering and building a nation while living by example.

Will I ever forget or dismiss the experiences I had growing up? No, but I now use my past as a guideline to what I strive to become and where I want to lead.

I am a woman with purpose, dignity, clarity, and flaws. I am not perfect, but I am a woman who is influential, and I know my worth. Before anyone decides to build wealth, including myself, I had to accept who I am.

What was the turning point that ignited the desire to live a wealthy lifestyle and what was the road traveled?

I was emotionally, financially, and mentally drained from the choices I made. I knew I deserved better and before I could receive whatever *it* was, I had to change.

I learned that knowledge and self-worth was going to give me an exceptional life. I am not an unintelligent individual by far, but I was falling into the same deteriorating routine each day. There was without a doubt a lack of motivation to seek change. I was perfectly fine with complaining and blaming my past for current mistakes.

The old blame game! It is so easy to blame your past for the decisions of today. The blame game was my safe exit. Day in and day out, I engaged in financial abuse. Yes, I abused myself.

Do you remember when I mentioned I saved over ten thousand dollars in my first 401k? The money never made it into the next retirement plan. When I left the job, I took the money with me instead of completing a rollover. I cashed the fund, then paid taxes and penalty. I did not care that I would have to start over.

I only saw thousands of dollars that would buy me what I wanted today. I was able to look good to others by splurging on friends and family without them knowing that I was neglecting myself.

I did not pay off my credit cards, loans, or deposit money into a savings account. I only cared about the moment and did not think about my future. I eventually realized that I was a victim of financial abuse. What made matters worse was that this behavior continued for years to come.

As women, you care for everyone else while placing your needs at the bottom of the list. Whether you live in the moment, give your last dollar to family, or neglect to secure a retirement fund…you are a victim of financial abuse.

One day, the abuse must come to an end. That is exactly what happened with me. I realized that when I changed one habit, it became a domino effect that protected my future.

One of the best behaviors that changed my life was positive thinking. I began to read books related to personal development.

Reading personal development books was a lifestyle change. If it was not related to my career, I was not engaging. I quickly had to change the course of my life...one book, one thought, and one habit at a time.

After reading statistics that categorized my lifestyle choices, I began to slowly change my habits towards a wealthy lifestyle.

One day well into my transformation years, I came across a fellow financial planner and author. Tom Corely is author of "Rich Habits." He shared 20 shocking differences in daily habits between poor and rich people.

There were two differences that stood out for me.

"Eighty four percent of wealthy people believe good habits create opportunity vs. 4% of poor and 86% of wealthy believe in lifelong educational self-improvement vs. 5% of poor."

It was another confirmation that I was on my way to building wealth. I also realized that my poor middle class behavior was due to personal habits, character, and choices.

You have a choice in life. It is your responsibility to acknowledge what it is that you want out of life and how to get there.

For years I knew my net worth; it was the self-worth that I struggled with. My acceptance came when I decided to acknowledge my self-worth and live the life I deserve.

Habit: Learn to create financial boundaries with self and others. Be content with who you are and what you have to offer life.

****

Clarity

****

"Never tell people how to do things. Tell them what to do and they will surprise you with their ingenuity." ~ George Patton

When my son was young, he would attempt to explain what he wanted served on his plate. We always allowed him to make his own decisions with our guidance of course. The problem occurred one time before dinner when his request was lost during delivery.

We eat plant-based meals, so his request was for "the green stuff and the orange stuff." After minutes of going through a list of vegetables, he became frustrated because I had no idea what he wanted. The loving conversation quickly spiraled into tears of confusion.

I use this example because so often we know what it is that we want, but neglect to properly convey it to others. When the other person does not deliver the message correctly, we become frustrated. This is true with how we treat ourselves. We want to be successful, but we do not articulate the steps to ourselves on how to get there.

Whether your message involves your dreams, goals, family, business, or money, you must be clear in whatever you seek.

You may wonder if dreams and goals are the same. They are not! Dreams are just wishing while goals are measurable tasks with a deadline. Goals have a due date.

Clarity begins with seeing the big picture exactly how you want and breaking down the vision into segments.

As a person who enjoys creating meals in the kitchen, I look at goals like a recipe.

When you are preparing a dish the recipe card will have the prep time, cook time, measurable ingredients, and steps for completion. It takes the guess work out of looking at the picture while trying to figure out how to make the dish.

Vision boards are the latest craze. But in order for the vision board to work, you must be willing to work as well. Visualize your goals, and then write down the steps you must take for your goals to come into fruition.

What dreams do you visualize that you want to turn into goals?

When dreams are the size of a

mustard seed and you have not made any moves, many wonder how they will get to the next level. Again, it all begins with clarity. You must indicate in a clear statement what you want in every aspect of your life in order to obtain success.

Each time I meet with clients, I request personal and financial goals. Too many times I hear, "I want to be debt free."

Although that is a great goal, it does not mean anything. In order to completely grasp and understand what you truly want, you must demonstrate clarity. Why? If not, you are not successful. Remember, you will receive what you articulate to others.

One year, I took my husband out to dinner for his birthday. Since he is truly predictable I knew which restaurant he would choose. It was one of his favorite places to eat and I was fortunate to have a gift card.

When the server arrived at our table she stated the specials along with the wine selection. Again, my husband is predictable, so I knew his special order. He turned to the server and requested the dinner portion Fettuccine Alfredo. I asked for Wheat Linguine pasta, bread sticks without salt, and a glass of water without ice and lemon wedges on the side.

As she proceeded to walk away, I asked her to repeat my husband's order. After repeating, my husband noticed she did not state exactly what he wanted. He always orders the dinner portion Fettuccine Alfredo, chicken, and spinach.

Had I not asked the server to repeat the order, the night would have had a different ending.

Life will give you exactly what you request. Even when you know what you want it is important to be clear to others in order to receive what you need.

Now, let us go back to the individuals who said, "I want to be debt free." To clarify exactly what is needed you must be more specific. A clear statement is, "I want to pay off $23,406.82 of consumer debt in three years by contributing $150 per week towards my balance."

You now have a specific plan that includes a timeline, measureable goal, and a plan for accountability. *A plan gives you power.*

Remember, everyone has a dream; it is how you take action that will allow your dreams to become goals.

Take the time to revisit your goals. Do your goals have a statement of clarity? Do your goals have a measurable timeline? Do your goals spell out its expectations?

> **Tip: Financial goals are just like personal goals, it needs work.**

By assigning a statement with clarity for your goals, you are being accountable. Now there is no excuse! We will visit accountability in more detail later in the book.

Have you ever wondered how you became consumed with debt? Do you ever stay up at night trying to figure out how to make ends meet?

There is a secret club, and everyone is invited. In other words, you are not the only one. I have met many who have fallen into the financial hole only to realize there is no one in yelling distance to hear their cries. After much discomfort, they come to realize that they have to rescue themselves out of debt.

When was the last time you gathered all your bills? Not only the ones you choose to open, **every** envelope that has your name including the bright past due stamp in the color of love (red).

It is time to have clarity about your debt. I know that debt is extremely emotional and at times can make you feel like a failure. This is the time to address the relationship you have with your debt and creditors. Gather all your debt and write down the total balance. Order all three credit reports [TransUnion, Equifax, & Experian] along with the FICO scores. Now add all the debt from each credit report.

What is your <u>magic</u> number? The magic number is how much you owe in debt. How do you feel about your number? For some of you it could be the very first time you are seeing this number. For others, it isno surprise. If it is no surprise, then why haven't you created a clear statement to eradicate?

Indicate how much you need to pay off (total) debt, designate a timeframe to pay off, and how much you will devote toward your debt every payday.

> **Tip: Designating a timeframe with a schedule will hold you accountable for the dollar amount you specify toward debt. The best way to remain focus is to open an account nickname "debt reduction" and auto transfer the specified amount into the account.**

Have you ever wondered how you arrived at your current position? You are not alone. Many people are thousands, even hundreds of thousands, in debt and have no idea where the funds were spent. It is even worse if you truly have nothing to show for your income. This is not to bash your financial mishaps, but to get you to realize that you are not taking complete responsibility for your finances.

Tip: Know your money, self- worth, and value.

To have clarity about your finances itis important to know your income, expenses, and contributions. It is also important to understand your well-being.

Ask yourself the following questions:

1. What is my gross income?
2. What is my net income?
3. How much am I contributing toward my retirement?
4. How much is going into a saving emergency fund?
5. Do I have a college savings plan?
6. What is my total liability?
7. How did I accumulate my debt?

8. What will I change about myself to pay off my debt?

In order to get an accurate understanding of your net income you should deduct your taxes, retirement, savings, and all expenses including commute (gas, parking, maintenance, train tickets), wardrobe, cleaners, daycare, and beauty/barber salon. The money you have left over after you have created your budget and paid every expense is your net income.

Yes, the definition of net income is different than what you have heard from other personal wealth experts. But when you consider a net income as how much you bring home, it actually is a true measure of the definition.

If you are creating a budget, every penny is accounted for before you bring home your paycheck.

Frightening, isn't it? Now you can see how important it is to eradicate your debt, cut expenses, and change your behavior.

The answers to these questions are imperative to address your financial state. I would like to embrace question #8.

What will I change about myself to pay off my debt?

I recall having the honor of working for an influential company. The company builds on great principles and it had a successful strategic plan to address the employees, customers, service, and products. There were multiple lines of businesses and teams within each district.

Although the company has a blue-print on how the company should conduct itself, the culture was primarily based on the management style of the Vice President.

The team members loved working for this particular company as it was shown by the integrity and longevity of employment. However, there were concerns that needed addressing. Each person was not as success-ful as his potential allowed him to be.

The team followed the rules, policies, and procedures, but the success rate was not up to standard. It was time to look into a change for each person.

The management considered positive reinforcement, but declined after noticing that after the employees received the reward the same behavior continued. It was time to discuss with each person what his expectations were from the company, his goals and how to address his attitude toward the workplace.

The Vice President knew it was easy to come into a workplace and set standards, but she wanted to make sure each person knew how to be successful daily by addressing their own needs.

In this case, management was the stem of the problem. Not because of her lack of management style, but because she was not clear as to what the team members needed from her. Having a successful team and home is indicative of self. To have proper interpersonal and intrapersonal communication will allow you to move forward.

The team members did not feel properly acknowledged and did not know where they were compared within the company. The reinforcements that were given were a great idea, but people did not know if it was because of individual success or the department success.

At that moment, she realized that she dropped the ball.

> **Tip: To address the problem, you need to know what the problem is.**

She was then aware that a change needed to occur with her and was willing to address each concern to have a successful team and self. Just then management knew she needed to understand what she expected from herself and to properly convey it to others. The time was a moment of clarity.

Just as you need clarity in the workplace to have a successful department, you also need clarity when it comes to your home and money.

Women are the first ones to sacrifice their future for others. If you do not indicate what you want in the home and workplace, you will find your demands are not being met because you never properly convey your expectations and approval.

Most of you have heard of the airplane analogy. The airline attendant explains that if there is an emergency, please put on your oxygen mask before you put on the oxygen mask of the person sitting next to you. Basically, take care of yourself before attending to someone else's needs.

As a mother and wife, this is extremely difficult to do because you want to make sure your children and spouse are taken care of before you are. Does this sound familiar?

How many parents are sacrificing their savings account, retirement plan, insurance and debt just to make sure the ones you love are secure?

Let me put this into perspective. There will come a time when it is too late for you to contribute towards your retirement plan because you have lost years to take advantage of compound interest. I understand that you want your children to play sports and join an activity. You even want to make sure your children do not have to worry about college. What about you?

You are spending thousands of dollars going above and beyond your means. Some of you are supporting adult children financially so they can maintain a certain lifestyle while your lifestyle diminish.

Do you want your children to live with insurmountable debt? Absolutely not, but you should not continue to spend your last dollar taking care of their wants and needs.

You cannot take out a loan for retirement and if you have an emergency, then you will have to request money from the same people you are supporting, which means that you will not receive a dime.

Now is the time to convey and demand what is expected from your family so that you are able to pay off your debt, accrue funds and build wealth.

Take the time to personally review your habits, how others may see you, and what needs to change.

(1) What have you noticed about your spending?

(2) What triggers your emotions?

Before you answer these questions take the time to ponder. You will be amazed how the answers affect you and the family you support.

The habits you practice now will become the habits you will continue during retirement.

One day, I was having a conversation with a client who was concerned with her father's finances. Normally I have direct consultation with the client, but I clearly saw she was extremely stressed.

She stated that she recently received a phone call from her sibling who wanted her to assist their father with his finances.

It seemed that their father was carelessly spending money and did not have a retirement fund. It was disturbing because he was 6 years away from retirement, plus he refinanced his home and purchased a new car.

When she asked her father about his finances, he told her he did not know the interest rate on his department store credit card.

He then explained that he refinanced his house after the interest rate dropped. The only good thing that he had was decent credit. Even though he did not have much to show for his hard work, he made sure the payments were always mailed in on time.

When it comes to your finances, it is important to know your total balance, interest rate, annual percent rate and terms.

I call this the 'car syndrome'. The car syndrome is when you go into the dealership and pretend you are not going to purchase a vehicle. At the end of a long day of negotiating, you walk out the dealership with a shiny new car, keys, and knowledge of monthly payment. That is how many people handle their finances. They are only concerned with the monthly payment.

They do not know their interest rate or the terms of the loan. They settle for the longest finance months in order to afford the monthly payment, not acknowledging the worth is less than what is owed in the end.

The father of the client handled all his finances with the 'car syndrome' approach. Unfortunately, this syndrome has multiple side effects. Although the daughter did not want to speak with her dad about his financial state, she had to.

First, she placed all his credit cards on the table to have a visual of what he had in his wallet. Then she collected the statements to highlight the ending balance and interest rate. The father was shocked because he never read anything outside the minimum requirement for the month.

The father indicated he knew there was a problem when he could not afford to purchase groceries and he made $85,000 annually. Does that sound familiar to any of you?

After the credit card intervention, it was time to discuss the mortgage. Seeking a lower interest rate is great, but you should always compare apples to apples.

Tip: Refinance your home with the same or lesser (timeline) term and better contract.

It turns out that her father lived in the home for 25 years. Wow, and still in tremendous debt due to consistent refinance! When he would refinance it would be for another 30-year term.

When you consider refinancing for a lower interest rate, it is important to know the length of the term you have on your existing contract.

To reap the benefits of the new agreement, you do not want to increase the timeline it takes to payoff the home.

Acknowledge where you are in your life and financial state. Stop going through the motions. Consciously read the terms and ask questions. Remember that even the most successful people need clarity when it comes to moving to the next task.

Workplace, home, and relationships involves having self-worth and putting your state of mind into perspective. Understand your purpose as to how to move forward in your endeavors.

Habit: Be specific about what you want
to accomplish, and the activities needed.
Acknowledge the habits that you must
change and enforce for success. Always
keep an open mind.

****

Leadership

****

"Do not follow where the path may lead. Go instead where there is no path and leave a trail." ~Harold R. McAlindon

Growing up I remember singing the song, *Three Blind Mice*. The problem with the mice was that they ran in multiples directions without a plan, resulting in their tails cut off. There was no plan of action, just the desire to get to a destination.

Luckily, the story ends with the mice using a tonic to grow new tails, learning a trade, recovering their eyesight, buying a house, and living happily ever after.

The blind mice strategy is how most households and businesses run their money. When there isn't a plan, difficult times occur and you realize that you must correct your mistakes so to live a happily life.

As much as I do not want to admit this, I started my company with the blind mice strategy.

> **Tip: To lead, you must first have an understanding.**

When I began my first company in 2008, I had no clue as to what I was doing. The *only* thing I did know was that I wanted to help people understand their money before managing their money. I did not want to become the blueprint financial firm where someone never considered your concerns, told you where to put your money for the sake of their commission, and then cut off communication once you left the office. I needed to implement coaching to get to know the clients, discuss their behaviors, and provide feasible strategies on how to discontinue malicious habits. There were not many women in the district who owned a financial firm, let alone actively coaching about finances to a marginalized community. Those who were well known in the field were hundreds of miles away and not in reach, literally and figuratively.

Before jumping out on faith, I remember having a conversation with my husband discussing how I wanted to become an entrepreneur. He asked to see a business plan. After showing him my plan he asked to see a contingent plan.

At the time I was offended because I thought I knew everything; I earned a MBA and worked in the industry for years.

After much conversation he explained that the plan looked great, but the timing was not right to begin a business. If you recall it was 2008, the beginning of the recession.

I agreed to delay the process for five years until one day I made an emotional decision.

At the time my son was involved in swimming. One Saturday I was able to take him to practice and watched along with the other parents. It was not until the end of the practice and meet when someone asked my son, "Who is that lady?" My son replied, "Bahiyah!"

The person asked again, "Who is she to you?" My son responded, "She's my mom!"

Can you believe how crushed my feelings were when this happened? I am the person who gave birth to him, rocked him to sleep, fed him in the middle of the night, and changed his diapers: I am his mother.

No one knew who I was because I worked countless hours for a company that wanted everything from me, including my peace of mind. Because of a demanding job, my husband was forced to be Mr. Mom.

At that moment I decided not to wait five years to start the business. It was going to happen sooner than later. I immediately went home and told my husband that I was putting in a notice to leave my position.

That was one of the longest nights of my life. Although my husband supports my decisions, this was one that he did not agree with, and it was not a secret.

Despite the lack of approval, I was now on my own. From the outside looking in, I had everything together. However, I needed someone to guide me through the process.

The quest to find someone as a mentor began.

I am an advocate on individuals having a mentor and coach. Both allow you to move toward an amazing life. Without a doubt, you must believe in you before someone will invest in you.

Have you ever wondered how others were able to catch a break before you? It is all in their belief. Your belief is that no one can replicate your talent. Belief captures passion, bravery, hope and determination.

There is no denying a person's belief in one-self.

I was driven to find the one person who had *it* and was not afraid of challenging me to bring out mine.

The more I searched for a mentor in my field, who was a trailblazer in the industry, the more I was introduced to men.

By no means am I expressing that women are not leaders; it seems that society does not take women as seriously as men when it comes to leading financial companies. It is so ironic, since women are the most influential demographics.

When you think about it, women have been the household CEO, CFA, CPA, social worker, teacher, secretary, bookkeeper, housekeeper, etc. for years.

We birth a nation! Women are leaders.

As time went on, I found women mentors that I was able to connect with through professional clubs, associations, committees, and social media outlets that I joined.

Although they were not in my line of work, they brought a different element to the table and I must say it was refreshing to have women who empowered each other and earnestly want to see you win.

I eventually surrounded myself with a positive group of women who were creating a path for themselves in their own fields. I not only had one mentor, but several. More importantly, we were mentors without claiming the title and adding pressure.

We supported each other, discussed ideas, and made sure each was performing as expected.

My search began seeking one individual only to realize that I first had to believe in myself, shed the fear of failing, and trust my decisions. *I then became the leader that I sought after.*

It is amazing how things work out in life. I have a new group of women who are like minded and support each other. Not to mention, we are all honest with expressing our opinions.

Believe me the leadership I received from them was useful during the time when my company was finding its way in a tough economy.

My consistency and interaction in the community allows me to prosper and share my experiences with other women.

Leadership is a privilege that many are honored to have but are not aware of the magnitude it entails. Never for a moment take your service for granted and do not stop sharing with others.

What are you sharing with other women? For me it is the following:

- You do not have to seek approval from anyone to be successful.
- You have to spend money to make money.
- You must secure your future.
- Be confident in making prudent decisions.

- Don't try to be everything to everyone.
- Seek assistance when needed.
- Keep an open mind.
- When you do well take someone with you.
- Define your success.

I quickly learned that leadership is not about who is at top of the corporate ladder. It is a person's way of engaging with others to share a vision and unite in quest of a common goal.

A leader follows a purpose. "Purpose leaders do not manage, leaders mesmerize. Leaders do not execute initiatives, they lead crusades.

Their brands are not labels but flags that should evoke the kind of patriotism we have for the countries we live in," Joey Reiman, CEO of BrightHouse.

You are a purpose leader. I am a purpose leader. Women are purpose leaders.

What crusade are you leading? Women are the most influential demographics. Therefore, women have the ability to lead by example. You have the power to show young men and ladies how to be respectful, listen, communicate, share, manage time, manage money, educate, be effective, work, have integrity, and ownership.

Live by the change you seek!

For me it took a few years to correct the mistakes I made, including starting a company during a recession. But today my husband and I agree it was the best decision.

Find your path and live it.

The next time you are discouraged think about one of my childhood sheroes, Sarah Breedlove, who made a way out of no way.

Sarah Breedlove was born on December 23, 1867, on a cotton plantation. Her parents were recently free slaves and Sarah was their fifth child. She was the first born as a freed slave. At the age of 7, Sarah became an orphan and was sent to live with her sister and brother-in-law in 1874. A few years later she began doing housework and picking cotton.

Can you imagine working from sunrise to sunset picking cotton? She was not the first in the family to perform such an act, but she made sure to definitely become the last. At this point, many would think their lives were already destined.

In 1881, Sarah married while escaping her oppressive environment. Shortly afterwards, she gave birth, her husband died, and she found work to pay for her daughter's education while attending night school herself.

One of the reasons why I admire Sarah is because she did not have time to make excuses. She had to make sure that she took care of her daughter and herself. She attended night school to further her education so that she was able to do better.

How many women put their lives on hold for the sake of someone else? The best gift you can ever give is taking care of self.

During the 1890s, Sarah developed a scalp disorder. Because of the disorder she lost much of her hair, so she began to experiment with treatments to improve her condition. Her treatments became successful, which allowed her to promote her products, give lectures, open a factory and a beauty school.

Sometimes in life you are given tests so that they turn into testimonies. Use your obstacles as stepping stones.

Today we know Sarah Breedlove as Madam C. J. Walker. If Madam C.J. Walker could pull herself out of a horrific situation, then you have no excuse. She became the first African-American female millionaire through her own business when it was unheard of at the time.

Madam C. J. Walker became a leader and will forever be a trailblazer. My suggestion to you is to go after what you desire.

Habit: Have a plan of action. Communicate and be honest with yourself and others. Learn to respect and have unwavering faith.

****

Education

****

"If you educate a man, you educate one person. If you educate a woman, you educate a nation." ~African Proverb

The benefit of educating women is felt throughout an entire community. An educated woman is able to educate her children, family, and others. Children who are well educated are mentally and physically healthy and likely to prosper with higher income.

The *Women in America*[i] report describes levels and trends in women's educational attainment, school enrollment, and fields of study. The data are primarily from the National Center for Education Statistics[ii] or the National Science Foundation[iii].

The report indicates regarding education:

• Women's gains in educational attainment have significantly outpaced those of men over the last 40 years. Today, younger women are more likely to graduate from college than are men and are more likely to hold a graduate school degree. Higher percentages of women than men have at least a high school education, and higher percentages of women than men participate in adult education.

• Educational gains among women relative to men can be seen across racial and ethnic groups and this trend is also present in other developed countries.

• Despite these gains in graduation rates, differences remain in the relative performance of female and male students at younger ages, with girls scoring higher than boys on reading assessments and lower on math assessments.

•   These differences can be seen in the fields that women pursue in college; female students are less well represented than men in science and technology-related fields, which typically lead to higher paying occupations.

As explained in the study, women are excelling in education. It clearly shows how women can make a major impact in the household by sharing their knowledge. The responsibility that is placed on females' shoulders begin during early childhood.

Throughout childhood most females are taught that to be successful they must be beautiful, supportive, and educated.

As effortless as it is for many to say that education does not come easy for some because of diminishing living conditions, there are women constantly fighting the stereotypes presented to them each day. However, there are many women who are casuality to financial warfare.

What can society do for women by teaching them how to properly manage money?

Women can improve the economy, one household at a time through the education of introducing financial planning instead of focusing so much on other things that are considered feminine.

One year I was honored to teach at a community college which was was the beginning of my adjct faculty journey. It was an experience that I will never forget and was excited to have had the opportunity. Rest assure, the position taught me things that I never knew about myself along with acquiring more patience.

One day before class began, I overheard a female student mention that she was going to receive a refund from the treasury office because of overpayment of a student loan. She was going to receive a check for nearly $5,000. Instead of declining the check, depositing into a savings account, or opening a Roth IRA she decided to purchase clothes, designer handbags, shoes, a phone, and rims for her boyfriend's car.

Can you imagine the frustration I felt when I overheard the conversation? This young lady decided to define her worth through material possessions and providing for her boyfriend instead of receiving monetary gain from investments.

Her behavior was a trickle effect that will characterize many households.

Her income did not support the decisions she made with the payment from school. She was clearly living in the moment.

Unfortunately, it is not solely the student's fault because the system is failing when it comes to bringing financial education to women and impoverished neighborhoods.

Let me make an announcement:

- ➢ If your purse costs more than the contents inside, you should not buy the purse.
- ➢ If your shoe collection is valued more than your financial portfolio, then your priorities are misplaced.
- ➢ If you know who Ralph Lauren is and not a Roth IRA, then you must immediately speak with a financial advisor.
- ➢ If you have convinced your legacy of females that a man will take care of you, then you are mistaken.
- ➢ If you have only saved money for holidays and school

clothing, then you must immediately create an emergency fund.

➤ If your only emergency fund is credit cards, then it is time to burn the plastic.

➤ If you refuse to work weekends because you do not want to miss a party, then your priorities are not in order.

➤ If you use a currency exchange for banking purposes, you must immediately research a financial institution in your area.

I have always wondered why most school districts focus on subjects other than personal finance. It is as if the boards of education feel that students will miracously understand how to manage money once they reach eighteen.

Newsflash! There is not a switch a person can flick to understand how to budget, save, invest, improve self-worth, and become entrepreneurs. Understanding of the topics mentioned is a lifelong process that must begin during youth.

To most educators, sex education seems more important than personal finance. The topic of sex is everywhere. The only thing I notice that is televised about money is the use of services after you make financial mistakes.

One day I was channel-surfing and noticed the commercials. Outside of previews, you will notice erectile dysfunction (ED), personal injury attorneys, bankruptcy, and credit card rewards.

You might think bankruptcy and credit cards are a form of financial education. In fact, you are wrong.

Although credit cards can help build and maintain your credit, the commercials never mention credit responsibility to the consumer. Instead, commercials correlate credit cards as a means to purchase items you may not have been able to afford otherwise. Once you charge your way into a deep financial hole, bankruptcy attorneys and debt consolidators are to the rescue. There is not mention about money management.

How many times have you used a credit card to make ends meet, purchase a gift, or as a form of bill payment?

Again, as the numbers for women increase for college enrollment and graduation, there is not a mention of mandatory personal finance courses. "When you teach a woman, you teach a nation."

Why do you suppose this is the case? It is simple, Oprah Winfrey said, "When you know better you do better."

If we had a nation of educated consumers the economy would not benefit from predatory interest rates, late payments and over limit fees. Would the economy still be able to exceed growth? Yes, it would. The economy would grow simply by the purchases made by consumers not by the financial mistakes of the consumers.

Financial prudency is learned.

I have researched numerous school districts to document the ones that have a personal finance or money management program established. What I have noticed is that many schools would rather discuss abstinence instead of proper money management. I can only assume educators are implementing abstinence when it comes to personal finance. The concept ***if you don't discuss the problem, a problem does not exist*** is apparently practiced by many.

On the contrary when you refrain from discussing the fundamentals of personal finance that includes banking, savings, retirement, and budget you neglect to educate a nation that is wise beyond its years.

If you do not agree, let us take a look at the existing and previous Presidential Administrations and Congress. The decisions made on behalf of the nation and continual permission of increasing the debt ceiling is not an example that should be led by anyone.

Imagine if your personal debt ceiling was increased, but your income remained the same. You would have the available credit accessible, which means you may use it only to find it difficult to repay your loans because you have increased your expenses without having enough money for repayment.

As households seek guidance from the Government, in most cases, the economy is worsening.

What that means is if the Government makes failed financial decisions by borrowing more than it can handle, default on loans and lower its credit rating so will each household without hesitation or accountability.

It is a prime example of leading by example.

<u>Congressional Budget:</u>

During the 1st quarter of 2012, the Senate voted and passed to allow a further increase in the debt ceiling. The vote allowed President Obama and administration to borrow $1.2 trillion more to operate a government that spent and mismanaged more than 55 percent than collected in revenue the previous year.

The debt ceiling immediately rose from $15.2 trillion to $16.4 trillion. The U.S. must get federal borrowing under control. Both its deficit and liabilities are higher as a percentage of gross GDP than some foreign countries.

If the government is not able to borrow more money, spending will have to be reduced to the amount of revenue the government has. *Translation: No increase in debt ceiling plus no spending equals acknowledge of budget.*

Many would dispute the government was waiting to collect funds that were owed to them. Until then, bills were scheduled to be paid while the interest was accumulating. The credit of the United States was in jeopardy.

Now, let us pretend that your household functioned like the government. Your household received $250,000 in a line of credit. Instead of paying your bills and investing, you decide to use the money toward vacations, luxury vehicles, clothing, accessories, golf clubs, memberships, and homes. You now realized that you have not paid off any debt, you actually added to what you currently have.

You then place a call to your lender and request an additional $250,000 because you mismanaged your funds and were late on a few payments. What would you think the lender would say?

How many are living wall to wall credit just to remain afloat with hopes that someone grants them more money?

How many women are in debt due to student loans, impulsive purchases, and spending to impress others?

There's much to learn from this situation.

Households:

1. Never spend your paycheck before receiving.

2. Work within your budget.

3. You cannot contact your creditors & request an increase in credit line when you're in default.

4. Not paying your bills on time will jeopardize your FICO score and reputation.

I strongly suggest that you take the time to educate yourself about your money. There are too many resources for anyone to use the excuse of not knowing.

Where can you get your financial education since it is not offered in school? You can receive your knowledge through experience, publication, media, coaching, and financial planning.

Take the steps to familiarize yourself with the economy and your money.

What is the debt ceiling?

What is your personal debt ceiling?

What is your debt to income ratio?

If your ratio is:

- <u>*30% or less*</u>*: This is a healthy debt load to carry for most households.*

- <u>*31%-49%*</u>*: You are on the road leading toward trouble unless you take action and responsibility. Find out why you're spending more than your income will allow.*

- <u>*50% or more*</u>*: Red Alert! You have made the wrong financial decisions. Your lifestyle is spiraling out of* *control. It is time to change how you feel about yourself and how you manage your money.*

Foreclosure Statistic:

Through the 1st quarter of 2012, there were 198,000 completed foreclosures compared to 232,000 through the 1st quarter 2011. Since the start of the financial crisis in September 2008, there have been approximately 3.5 million completed foreclosures.

Approximately 1.4 million homes, or 3.4 percent of all homes with a mortgage, were in the national foreclosure inventory as of March 2012 compared to 1.5 million, or 3.5 percent, in March 2012 and 1.4 million, or 3.4 percent, in February 2012.

The number of loans in the foreclosure inventory decreased by nearly 100,000, or 6.0 percent, in March 2012 compare to March 2011.[iv]

Most of the reckless financial decisions began with the housing market. Prior to 2008, investors and homeowners were purchasing more housing than each could actually afford. It sounded like a great idea.

The market value was up, interest rates were low, and everyone was approved.

Today, many are crushed by the decision made years ago. When subprime lending occurred, this was making loans to people who may have difficulty maintaining the repayment schedule; no one ever imagined the outcome.

Most new buyers were so elated to be approved and own a home no one actually read the terms. One could only wonder why, when the housing market dropped in value, you were approved, yet your income remained the same. Surely, you would be able to afford the monthly notes…right?

Wrong!

Most lenders did not take the time to acknowledge and explain the low interest rate was fixed for two years with a variable interest rate afterwards. Many borrowers would have thought twice about signing their name on the dotted line.

For most, it is not solely the value of the home that is damaging the borrowers; it is the increase in monthly payment.

Do you see how an education in mortgage payments is needed?

The income did not change but the mortgage note increased by $600 or more. The increase in payment was not budgeted during the closing. If so, the borrowers could have either refinanced for a fixed interest from an adjustable interest or reconsidered altogether.

The economy, consumer spending, debt ceiling, personal debt ceiling, and stock market all have to do with education.

Take matters into your own hands by reading about what is happening with your money. Again, there are too many resources available such as CNN Money, Bloomberg, Kiplinger, Black Enterprise, and other educational media outlets.

Habit: Read 30 minutes a day to improve your knowledge of financial empowerment. Share your experience.

****

Accountability

****

"Restoring responsibility and accountability is essential to the economic and fiscal health of our nation." ~ Carl Levin

The most successful women have direction, clarity, adaptability, and accountability. The business strategy each practice is equally important in a personal position.

Where do you want your experiences to take you? Life is a journey, and it is your responsibility to enjoy the moments, journal your lessons and accept nothing but the best for and from yourself. Success is intentional never accidental. How many roads have you traveled only to notice that it was not the road intended? Although you did not plan to travel the road to reach your goal it was intentional for you to learn the lessons needed. Whether the lessons were for you or for you to share with others, you needed it. Now, share the wealth.

Who have you allowed on your team? Your friends and family are the influencers of your thoughts and actions. They will either encourage you or break your spirit when it comes to hope. Make sure to surround yourself with like minds who are challenging you.

Are you the person who will rise to the occasion when needed? Do you set dead-lines for your goals and find ways to achieve by any means necessary? Do you allow the opinions of others to stop your success? Obstacles happen in life. If obstacles did not occur everyone would wake up and accomplish every thought, wish, and goal for the day. Life does not happen that way, so in order to have a piece of success you will engage in some complication. The best solution for you is to make sure that you can adapt to your environment. Always be flexible with your attitude and approach. The ones who fail often are the ones who are not able to conform to change while holding themselves accountable. Let me clarify that we all fail. I am referring to failure resulting in defeat because you were not willing to step outside the box or pick it up and run with it.

Believe it or not, accountability has everything to do with both money and maturity. You are accountable through the habits you form throughout life.

Kathy Kaehler is an author, celebrity trainer, spokesperson and mom who devotes her career to helping people live happy, productive and healthy lives. Beyond teaching the latest in fitness workouts with celebrities and appearing on the Today Show this lifestyle expert focuses on success through accountability.

"Accountability is an old-fashioned idea that says you are responsible for your actions. The willingness to be accountable for what you do, what you do not do or refuse to do is a significant trait of your character", says Kathy Kaehler.

Let us face it when it comes to goals most people stop with a dream. Many never take the time to implement a plan, write out the details, the due dates, and recruit a partner, if needed.

Recently, I met a lady who was successful in her line of work but was not happy. She explained how she lacked satisfaction with her career because it was no longer gratifying, and she did nott have time to do what truly brought her happiness. In case you are wondering, she earned a six figure salary. However, she was willing to quit her profession without any notice and adequate saving. Did I mention that she wants to change to a field with absolutely no experience?

She is a prime example that it does not matter how much you earn. When you are not living a life of wealth and purpose, you are not building a legacy.

I began asking the following questions:

1. What are your dreams?
2. What goals do you have in place?

3. Do you know exactly what you want in life?

4. Why did you choose this career?

5. Have you given yourself a deadline?

6. Have you researched what is required?

7. Do you have any options?

8. What accountability system is in place?

It was clear that she is seeking happiness, but she has not given any thought as to how to fulfill her dreams. She only had a desire to do better.

To do better, you must be willing to do things that ordinary people are afraid to do. As simple as it sounds, most people do not want to put in the work it takes to be successful.

Success does not occur overnight. As a matter of fact, people have been working on their skills for years only to be prepared when opportunity knocked at a chance to prove themselves.

From time to time, I like to read about the success of people who are where I want to be in life.

Let us take a look at some of the world's richest women.

The list of billionaires increased for women from 104 in 2012, 138 in 2013 to 172 in 2014. Do you think the list happened by chance? No, it was intentional due to the practices mentioned at the beginning of this chapter.

Each woman decided to let go from abuse of procrastination. This abuse is the practicality that you allow fear to paralyze your dreams from turning into reality because you lack the action to plan out your future. Trust me, one day it will be too late. Make sure that day does not come for you.

The following women made sure to create a plan to reach success with their own expectations in mind.

Top five: World's Richest Women[v]

1. Christy Walton ($38.2 B)

2. Alice Walton ($35.5 B)

3. Liliane Bettencourt ($35.3 B)

4. Jacqueline Badger Mars ($20.2 B)

5. Susanne Klatten ($18.4 B)

Top three: World's Richest Black Women

1. Isabel dos Santos ($3.7 B)

2. Oprah Winfrey ($2.9 B)

3. Folorunsho Alakia ($2.5 B)

There are a few names that you may be familiar with due to popularity. For me, Folorunsho Alakia (b. 1951) replicates the behavioral pattern of women who desire to be their own boss. She began her career in 1974 as an executive secretary in the banking industry.

Alakia did not allow her secretarial position to limit her goal to a wealthy life. As a matter of fact, she did not attend a college or university. She insisted that a formal education was not required to have a successful life. I am not indicating that higher education is not important. I am stating that you should never use lack of formal education or the opinion of someone else as an excuse for not going after your dreams.

If you are privilege enough to graduate from college, use it to the best of your ability, but never as an abuse of procrastination.

Alakia furthered her career in the banking industry where she worked before establishing a tailoring company, Supreme Stitches. Her company eventually became a household name and she worked hard to further her plans while promoting fashion.

Nearly twenty years later in 1993 she acquired an oil prospecting license, which granted her a block in Nigeria's coastal water. Alakia partnered with Texaco to explore her block and in the year 2000, they discovered a one billion barrel oil field. She now holds sixty percent stake in the oil field. As you can see Alakia's success did not occur over night.

How many of you are currently employed and dreaming of moving on to establish your company? How many of you are just like the lady mentioned earlier in this chapter who has a desire to switch industries, but has no idea where or how to begin?

Sometimes, you use your current role to mold your behavior, establish connections and finance your goals.

There is a lot to learn from Alakia, one of the richest black women in the world.

(1) Never allow your current state dictate your future.

(2) You do not have to live in the delusion of others, but in the reality of your destiny.

(3) Have a goal in mind and take the steps to accomplish.

Whether you want to own a business, create a website, get out of debt, or make more money it begins with a plan followed by accountability.

Remember, abuse of procrastination will rob you of success each time. The best way to hold yourself accountable is to write down due dates for your goals. If the goals do not happen when you plan just adjust the date along with your attitude and approach. More importantly, be precise with your goals.

If you are walking in a state of confusion, then is it possible you will not have clarity of success.

Habit: Write your goal on a calendar with a task to complete each day. Make sure it is clear and concise. Break down the goal with actions, deadlines, and amount of money needed. Set an alarm as a reminder to work. Place your goal where it is visible and view daily.

****

Save your future

****

"Do not save what is left after spending but spend what is left after saving." ~Warren Buffett

Women will give their last dollar to everyone else, but when it comes to themselves, the ball falls short. Why do you suppose women feel less deserving than others? Some would argue that it is the role of a woman to nurture. Let us clarify that nurturing others does not mean neglecting yourself. If you truly believe that you are worthy, you will not dare put yourself last. The best way to present yourself is when you are enthusiastic, enlightened, educated and excited because you have taken steps to supply all your needs.

Only then will you be capable of doing the same for others.

Awhile back I sat down with a parent to discuss her retirement plan. She was a teacher for twenty-three years who took pride in instructing her students but was the first to admit that she had no idea how to manage money.

She recalled being taught that you must go to college, find a job, get a pension, get married, have children, buy a house, and then retire. Even after endless suggestions from friends and family about what she must do as an adult, no one ever mentioned the importance of saving for the future. Many were seeking employment with pension benefits.

Because of her lack of understanding of wealth, she would put money into a savings account and retirement fund only to withdraw later. She treated her savings as a piggy bank and her retirement fund as an emergency plan.

The teacher was never a student of financial literacy. She knew that her paycheck was a means to supply her needs but did not know how to allocate the funds. Unfortunately, her wants got in the way of reality.

As we continued to discuss the purpose of the meeting, she requested to take out a loan to pay for her son's freshmen year college tuition. She never prepared for the day by saving toward a College 529 Plan and did not want him to apply for student loans.

As an alternative, she was willing to go further into debt and abuse her retirement fund, instead of him graduating from college with student loan debt just as she did in the past. Let me make an announcement to all the parents who want to do the right thing for their children. The right thing to do for your children is to teach them how to save for the future. If you do not know how to do that yourself there is a plethora of resources available for the household to learn together. If not, you are teaching your children the lack of importance of financial prudence. This is a major mistake and a generational curse to having a dysfunctional relationship with money.

What this teaches the next generation is that it is acceptable to abuse the relationship with money, which results in neglect of self.

Obviously, I could not agree with her decision. So, I encouraged her to research other options. As much as it is a burden to accumulate student loans, it is even worse when you are not able to make ends meet during retirement. There is not a loan for that!

Women will discuss every topic except money. Why? People are either embarrassed, secretive, or fear what they do not know.

Because of the fear that women have with money, they are not able to negotiate higher salaries, lack adequate saving balances, and have higher credit card balances. Just think how much power women would have if more girl talks included ways to manage, save, and spend money. Not to mention, women would have considerable conversations amongst them-selves instead of having men attempt to understand a female point of view while providing suggestions.

Understanding and confronting your fear of money will shift you into financial success. First, discover what money means to you. It means different things to different people.

Money can represent love, happiness, power, fear, intimidation, control, or freedom. Many will say that money allows them the ability to purchase necessities. While others will point out that it's a tool necessary for success.

Second, find a way to lead by example. This would break the generational dysfunction with money. Children learn certain behavior from parents, guardians and influential members of the community.

How you handle your money is how your children will handle their money in the future. How many times have you done or said something that reflected on the behavior of your parent? That is how others, including your children, will think of you as you attempt to influence your household and community.

Knowing or not, you are possibly teaching your children to live a neglectful lifestyle. When you decide to purchase your wants before your needs, that is neglect. Until you change your behavior and openly discuss with your children how to properly handle their finances everyone will continue to have a broke mentality.

Lesson: How to teach children the value of money

Studies have shown that most learn through visual tactics instead of auditory. We have all heard our parents say, "I *preached* until I was blue in the face"---that's auditory.

Before you begin to change colors from disappointment consider ways to teach your children the value of money.

Take your children to the store with a list of items and a stipend. Make sure the list includes items from grocery to clothing. The goal is to show your children how to function within a budget, pay attention to brands, and acknowledge the value of items.

While shopping with your children explain to them the difference in value and the reason why you would choose a particular item over the others. As a parent, it is easy for you to tell your children to pick up a specific item or even say 'no' to their requests, but when you begin to explain your intentions behind each decision the process of valuing money becomes clear.

This is a lesson that I created specifically, for workshops. This example encourages parents to show their children the value of money.

How often have we read about entertainers and athletes becoming financially destitute after earning millions over the years?

The most impactful story I read was about an NFL athlete, Chris McAlister, who signed a seven year extension contract with the Baltimore Ravens in 2004 for $55 million. He played for five years before released to the Saints where he eventually retired. That amount of money would allow you to accomplish all your goals from a means to an end to purchasing all needs including wants.

To my dismay I learned, that in 2011 he was living with his parents while they were supplying his basic living needs. He was also pleading with the courts to lower his child support because he did not have money. How could anyone spend $55M in less than ten years better yet a lifetime? Easily, when you have a broke mentality your behavior is difficult to change. Not impossible, but difficult!

Many people truly believe that once you receive an enormous amount of money your dreams will miraculously come true. That is not the case. If you never change your behavior and educate yourself, expect the same results.

> **Tip: Money is not the root of evil. Money is not the root of happiness. It is the beginning of possibilities.**

If you are accustomed to spending money as soon as you receive it, you will do the same with $1.00 or $1,000,000. Let me repeat---if you do not change your behavior and attitude about how you treat $1.00. You will act the same if you were to earn your ideal income. The keys are to account for each dollar, hold oneself accountable to what you plan to do with your money, and practice positive habits. The billionaires you read about in the previous chapter not only held themselves accountable with their goals, but their money too.

No one plans to go broke, but your behavior and practice will lead you toward that path if you are not careful. Chris McAlister is not the only person to have lost millions due to mismanagement of money.

A person I admire dearly, Iyanla Vanzant, also had the misfortune of losing her fortune. In Ms. Vanzant's case it was due to lack of education. While going through life's changes she signed a contract with a balloon mortgage payment.

A balloon mortgage is when the last payment is an outstanding amount (i.e. 359 payments for $675.00: last payment for $36,325). Again, it is important to read the terms of your contract so that you can save your future. Take your time, read your terms, and comprehend what you're signing.

Mismanagement, lack of preparation, scarce education, and losing your money is devastating to your spirit and self-worth. However, it is a message that can be shared with many. Your situation is available for others to use as a guideline to make prudent decisions.

How can you lead with your finances? When you understand your current situation you're able to be aware of your future.

After you indicate exactly what you expect from yourself, it is time to create a plan also known as a budget. This is nothing to be ashamed of.

There are two misconceptions on why consumers create a budget plan.

(1) You do not have *any* money and may consider bankruptcy.

(2) It is for those who do not have *enough* money to purchase what they need.

Tip: The origin of our word budget is the Latin <u>bulga</u>, a little pouch or knapsack, which may have come from a Ghoulish source that's related to the Irish <u>bolg</u>, "bag". (Quinion 1998)

According to the origin of budget, it is a little pouch. If you were obligated to spend only what you could carry, then you had no choice but to live within your means.

Think of your budget as 'use it or lose it' for what you have available. Currently, we reference a budget as a financial document used to project future income and expenses.

The process for preparing a budget includes:

- Listing of all sources of income
- Listing of all required expenses
- Listing of retirement and savings
- Listing of other possible activities

In order to get to a destination, you must know how to get there.

I remember being asked to speak at a conference. The leadership conference consisted of a group of successful women who were well established in their career. The topic of conversation was, "The importance of setting and reaching your goals." It did not take much consideration to agree to the terms and arrange transportation. The location was far, but not far enough to schedule a flight. The travel time was about 2 hours.

Since I always factor in time and distance when negotiating a fee, I knew how much was allocated toward travel from my pay. The navigation system listed the travel time, mileage, and distance travel. After each command to turn, the navigation would display the mileage traveled.

This display was helpful because it also allowed me to calculate how much further I would drive until I needed to fill up another tank of gas. Once I reached my destination the system indicated I had arrived with the complete mileage and time displayed. It was exactly what I originally calculated.

Your 'use it or lose it' plan is similar to a navigation system. A plan tells you how far you are able to travel, how much you would need for expenses and how long it would take to reach your destination. If you go through life without a plan you will end up like a person without a navigation system…wondering which way to turn. If you do not believe me, recall the conversation and articles read about multiple athletes and entertainers who are now without finances to pay for their basic living needs. Neither one knew the importance of a plan.

> **Tip: It does not matter how much money you earn. It matters how much money you spend.**

Once a plan is complete with all your expenses including mortgages, utilities, gas, retirement, savings, insurance, date night, grooming, etc. you must stick with your action plan. Again, what you do not plan or use, you will lose due to mismanagement. Do not forget to list your goals as well. Listing your goals will motivate you to stay on track.

Again, women are influential in household spending. Once you are able to get a grasp on where to allocate monies, you will be able to save toward your future and build wealth. That is part of the use it plan.

Do you remember when we discussed the origin of budget, which was a little pouch? Great I challenge you to create a little pouch, or an envelope.

Place cash in an envelope for variables like, entertainment/ activities, lunch, gas, date nights, grooming, etc.

Paying with cash allows you to keep track of your money. If you notice that you have depleted all the money inside the envelope then you are not able to engage in the activity. The cash envelope system forces you to hold yourself accountable.

In fact, between 1989 and 2006, Americans' overall credit card debt grew by 315 percent from $211 billion to $876 billion. [vi]

The increase in credit card debt demonstrated the dyfunctional relationship with money that most consumers had and currently practice.

If half the consumers relied on a 'use it or lose it' plan instead of revolving credit, the overall credit card debt would be much lesser because they planned for purchases and activities. Practice your plan with less credit and more cash as guidance to save your future.

You will be amazed how far your financial navigation system will allow you to travel. It is imperative you visit your plan each day as a reminder of goals or you will lose focus and your money. Do not make the mistake of over thinking. Do as you plan and move on.

Once you grasp the concept of income, expenses and needs you should invite the family for an educational session.

Why, you wonder? Because you are a leader and leaders share their wisdom.

Contribute to your household and community. Your knowledge will allow others to encourage and strengthen the belief in oneself. Unfortunately, many people think they are alone, which is not the case.

Habit: Create a plan that includes a contribution towards debt elimination and saving/retirement. Make sure to account for every penny. Instead of using credit cards for impulsive purchases, emergencies, sales items and bill payments, use cash. Ask yourself questions before making decisions about your money. (i.e. Will this decision get me closer to <u>my</u> goals?) If not, then do not do it.

****

Supportive

****

"It's about women helping women and doing things together and supporting each other." ~Diana Burch

Complimenting and supporting someone else's talents does not take away from your gifts. It is time to realize that you can go much further working together rather than waiting for someone to fall. It is the difference between empowerment and competition.

This also distinguishes the strengths within you.

Hillary Rodham Clinton once said, "Women are the world's most underused resource." One of the reasons why this is so profound is because there is validity in the statement. Women often neglect to rely on each other to help reach their goals and often times ignore the possibilities in the grand scheme of things.

Is it probable to build a supportive team? Absolutely, but the team must begin with self.

Shonda Rhimes is a screenwriter, director, producer, and creator of multiple hit television shows and has found a way to show millions of weekly viewers that when a woman is surrounded by a team, she is unstoppable. More importantly, when she believes in self and support her decisions there is not anything that can stand in the way.

Behind the scenes, Shonda has a creative team of writers who are relentless in making sure each show is equipped with suspense and drama. In front of the camera, she has managed to create several hit television shows, including Scandal, which presents a team starring Kerry Washington as Olivia Pope. Olivia is a political crisis management inspired by a real-life former press aide Judy Smith.

Her team of gladiators are individuals who bring their expertise to resolve a crisis that is presented to Olivia Pope by a person in desperate need of a resolution. It is clear that Olivia is capable of getting the job done alone, but with a support team who can handle the situation there is a better chance that the mission would be accomplished.

The reason why I bring up Scandal is because in spite of how smart and capable you are of achieving your goals, you need a team that will assist when needed, hold you accountable to the goal, and get it handled. It is your personal support group.

So, who is on your team? How are you supporting yourself? What steps are in place to make sure that you follow through with your goals?

Whether you are a business owner or not, you must think of yourself as the chief executive officer (CEO) of your success. This will include a personal mission statement, daily goals, plan, and a group to help execute.

The best collaboration is to begin with like minds of individuals who equally want to see you succeed. Let us start with the person in the mirror. Next, look at the people who are in your circle of friends and family. Lastly, branch out to other women who you admire and respect their strengths.

If you want to thrive, your environment must consist of leaders who play an intricate part in your success.

Too often, I hear women express that they can do it alone. They can pay their own bills, buy their own house, take care of their kids, start their own business and they can change their own tire. Why? It is because of the need to be independent instead of interdependent. Women were created to be supportive, innovative, astute, and beautiful, not strong. Do not confuse strong with persistence. Be flexible.

Independence is great, but even a successful leader of a country has an administration with a title and significant responsibilities. Productive administrations have regular meetings that will keep the entire team informed of issues, solve problems, and discuss ideas. This group holds the person in charge responsible for her actions and work beyond captive boundaries.

The main behavior to show support of self and others is to practice discipline. Discipline is needed to exercise when one has a mission to accomplish. Whether you want to get out of debt, start a company, write a book, or begin a course, it begins with a clear idea of your goal and what is expected.

Without discipline you lack support. You and your team must make sure that you are performing according to what is stated daily to zealously work toward the bigger picture.

Will everyone be able to work as a gladiator on your team? Absolutely not, but those you encounter must be able to play an important role where you are able to learn, grow, and share.

Habit: Join a group, whether professional, mastermind or meet up, to affiliate self with individuals who have similar goals. Form relationships to continue discussion of plans. Your group should be more excited about your success than you. Stick with it!

****

Wealth Management

****

"A woman's best protection is a little money of her own" -Clare Boothe Luce

Earlier I mentioned discussing about a retirement plan with a teacher who invested in a retirement savings for twenty-three years only to find out that she wanted to take out a loan to help her son pay for college. For me, wealth means wholeheartedly engaging in activities leading to (financial) happiness. For others, wealth means accumulating funds leading towards financial security. Either way, one must make sure the actions coincide with the goals.

A person cannot secure a future if the actions are neglectful. Too often, women are overwhelmed with taking care of others while putting their needs last. Planning for their future takes a back seat in life. But the day must come when self is precedence.

Financial planning is frequently mentioned without a clear understanding of what it is or how to accomplish it.

In the early 1990s, I scheduled an appointment to see a financial advisor at A.G. Edwards. I remember walking into a huge lobby with a receptionist desk that was so intimidating in size with the only female in the office greeting everyone at the front door.

After introducing myself, I was told to have a seat and wait for the next available representative. After waiting nearly thirty minutes, I was greeted by a distinquished gentleman with a firm grip and a smile that screamed m-o-n-e-y. We slowly walked down the long hallway into an oversized room filled with plaques and certificates.

The advisor began telling me about the company and himself. He eventually asked what assets I owned and how much money I had to invest.

This was my first interaction with an advisor. The meeting was impersonal, and I did not feel as if he took the time to learn about my needs and explain what I needed to know as a young investor. I was clearly a commission check to him. At that moment, I realized that I did not have any assets. I only knew that I wanted to have a retirement plan since I read that the earlier you began, the better off you were in the future. The only asset I had at the time was my college education and a used vehicle that was not worth mentioning.

Each question he asked was followed by a "No". At the time, I did not own a home, stock, bond, mutual funds, certificate of deposits, commodities, insurance policies, antiques, or jewelry.

As I sat in his office, I felt the hope of wealth management dissipate from my plans. Since I did not have much money to invest, I was denied a financial portfolio. The advisor did not take the time to guide me into the direction of a firm who would be willing to start with a small deposit and monthly contributions.

How many of you can relate to feeling as if you cannot afford to invest in your financial future? Consumers have been misled to believe that you must have a lot of money to make money. That is not the case. Wealth management is simply combining personal investment management, financial planning, and disciplines for the benefit on increasing net worth. I was determined to combine my disciplines with a portfolio. My goals were more than the label he placed on me and what he could not vision.

As a young investor the meeting could have gone into a different direction to guide me toward a profitable future. Instead, I was told that I did not have anything to invest.

Imagine how many women are treated as if they do not have anything to offer. Whether it is your dollar, time, ideas, or efforts, each is valuable and can be applied toward financial wealth.

Before you can invest in a financial plan you must begin with support through discipline. What have you trained yourself to do in order to accomplish specific goals?

What some women are not taught is that the same discipline you use to manage your household and reduce debt is the same discipline it will take to manage a financial plan.

Ask yourself, "What would you like for your money to do for you?" Make sure your response is clear and measurable. Had I been asked this question when I met with an advisor from A.G. Edwards, I would have responded that "I want to save $2 million to secure my lifestyle when I retire at 65 years old. I want my money to grow during my working years by aggressively investing while making monthly contributions of $250." It is unfortunate that the advisor and I never had that conversation.

I am glad to say that because I continued to use the resources that were available to me I was able to control my destiny. I began investing on my own and through my employer. In life, successful people create their own opportunities instead of waiting for others to present it to them. You must become an advocate for self and never take someone else's doubt or opinion as an acceptance for your future.

Your financial plan can begin with simply opening deposit accounts (checking account & saving). There is not a magic pill or a light switch for success. This clearly is not the Matrix. It takes time, patience, and discipline. Remember, how you behave in one situation is how you will behave in another situation. Therefore, if you are not able to properly manage your deposit accounts, then you will not be able to manage your investment accounts and insurance policies.

As simple as this sounds, society is not doing a great job with conveying this message to young investors and women to properly prepare them for challenges while building wealth. You can get ready for your future by acknowledging the obstacles and following the solutions.

Types of bumps on a financial path:

1. Spend more than you earn.

2. Save less than eight months of expenses.

3. Neglect your retirement plan.

4. Constant worry about finances.

5. Avoid a written financial plan.

The road leading toward a secure future will not be easy. At times, you will want to take the road most traveled. However, that road is consumed with debt and doubt. Why not plan for what is to come?

Ways to detour to success on a financial path:

1. Be honest about where you are.

2. Be clear about where you want to be.

3. Create a use it or lose it plan & stick with it.

4. Create an emergency fund.

5. Educate self about money management, and then do it.

How many bumps have you encountered beginning with someone not believing in your abilities? For some, the answer is more than you would like to admit.

Because of my personal experiences and encounters with others has led me to become the person I am today, who service many while educating on how to reach goals by holding everyone accountable while building self-worth and networth.

One day I met with a client name Christina. She was impressionable in a tailored outfit, heels, and a clutch purse. She was also well poised, well spoken in the conversation, and excited about discussing her accomplishments. Christina revealed that she wanted to create a portfolio but did not know where to begin. Now that I was the person asking questions, I made sure to ask about her goals, habits, and past experiences, instead of focusing solely on assets.

After speaking with Christina for nearly forty minutes it was clear that she wanted financial freedom. Anyone looking at her would have assumed that she lived a lucrative lifestyle. Although she did, the lifestyle was distracting from her goals.

Financial freedom is more than money in your pocket. It is maintaining a comfortable lifestyle through eliminating debt and saving for your future, which results in a peace of mind. Financial freedom *is* peace of mind. Whether you earn five, six, or seven figures everyone wants to have peace.

Following the meeting, Christina pulled me to the side to explain that she has a great home and job but wanted more. Throughout her life she was told that she could either have a career or family but could not achieve both. As disturbing as the previous comment sounds, many women have been told that they must choose between the two because it would be impossible to excel in both.

If women are driven to earn a living they are labeled as assertive. If women decide to put family first, then they are labeled as a homemaker. Why aren't men labeled as such? More women are refusing to believe they must choose between suitable careers and loving homes. As difficult as it is at times, many are practicing the art of balance.

My goal was to reassure Christina that she could have financial freedom through wealth management and abolish the myths.

Tip: If you do not like where you are in life do something about it. Do not complain. Do not wish. Do not hope. Just make it happen.

Here are steps that I encourage you to practice if you want more out of life, which I am sure you do:

Have a conversation with your spouse regarding goals. Whether you are married, have a partner or single, you must discuss your aspirations, expectations from self and others, create a plan, and stick with it.

Manage the deposit accounts.

Use your checking account as a record to compare against your budget to track your spending and hold you accountable. Set reminders to pay your bills prior to the due date while creating a debt elimination plan. Maximize your saving account by arranging an automatic payroll deposit to remove the responsibility of having to do it yourself.

Gather all financial statements.

Knowing where your accounts stand is winning the battle against financial war. Too often, consumers are not aware of how much they owe, the annual percentage rate, and minimum payment required. Collect all your statements and carefully document where you stand with each account. Make sure to store and organize the statements in a place that is easily accessible.

Take advantage of an employer-sponsored retirement plan. Why leave money on the table? If your employer offers to match your contribution, it is your financial best interest to take advantage of the "free" money. The contributions are pre-tax and tax deferred, so you will not miss as much as expected. Begin with contributing the match amount from your employer. For example, if an employer matches one hundred percent of the first three percent, then that is the amount you should begin. Each year, increase your retirement contribution by the amount you are rewarded as a raise. You will be able to maximize your raise through an investment instead of opting to receive in your payroll.

Open a Roth IRA account. The contributions to the Roth IRA are with after-tax
funds. A Roth IRA is an individual
retirement account that offers a valuable tax
break. The account contains investments in
common stocks and bonds. It is ideal for
investors who have maxed out an
employer-sponsored plan and/or want to
invest with funds while taking advantage of
certain tax breaks.

Diversify your plan. Make sure to
make the most of your money. Too often,
investors make the mistake of diversifying
in companies instead of plans. Investors
want to make sure a portfolio is invested in
equities (large, mid, small, and international)
and bonds. While distinguishing between an
aggressive, moderate, conservative, or bal-
anced investor the allocation is driven by the

percentage of equities and bonds. Ideally, you do not want to have all your money in one basket.

Goals must relate to an investor's risk tolerance, time horizon, and attitude toward volatility. Do not allow an advisor to convince you to invest in a fund that does not feel comfortable to you. Keep in mind that it is your money, and you should ask as many questions as possible to make sure that your goals are met.

Do not kick your fund when it is down. A sure way to lose most, if not all, your money is to close it out when the market is not doing well. Make sure to monitor the account to view how it is performing. If you do not like the results, wait until the market improves before moving the funds. The best practice is to ride out the storm and enjoy the ride.

Track the progress of a plan. Once you receive a plan of action for your portfolio make sure that it is implemented. This can easily occur by setting up the appropriate accounts, automate dollar cost average, and establish estate planning strategies.

Insure your life because you are worth it. Do not put the financial burden on your loved ones. Life insurance policies are not designed to make your beneficiary rich, but it will eliminate the stress of taking care of your affairs at your demise.

Statistically, women outlive men. Women should inquire about a long-term care insurance policy to cover in the event you need assisted living, home care, adult daycare, hospice care, and nursing home. Do not expect your children to willingly move you into their home.

Implement strategies that you can control. Financial plans are a great way to tap into the market, while taking advantage of earning higher interest rates. However, you can also welcome more money into the household with passive income and turning your hobbies into paid work. A lucrative business and passive income should pay you while you sleep. Everyone has a dream that they want to fulfill. Are you an expert? Do people come to you and ask questions? Do you have a book that you want to release? Is there a course that you want to teach? You do not have to wait for an invitation. Be pro-active about earning more money and create an e-course and write an e-book. This is ideal as passive income.

Reduce debt to have more cash flow. Since you have already gathered your statements and are aware of how much you owe it is easy for you to create a debt elimination plan beginning with the lowest balance. As you pay off each account you are then able to apply the payments toward the next one.

Save! Save! Save! There is a strategy that I created to 'Pay You First'. The goal is to change your discipline while increasing your saving account. First, calculate a sensible percentage of your net income. I suggest beginning with eight percent. Second, open a savings account that is not easily accessible. I recommend an online account to avoid frequent withdrawals. Lastly, complete a split deposit via human resources at your employer or set up an automatic transfer from checking into saving. Over time, you will notice an increase in the account. The percentage was recommended to demonstrate that you have the capability to save money and not allow excuses to get in the way of your goals. Over time, it is recommended that you increase the allocation. Ideally, you should increase by one percent every six months until you reach an ideal percentage.

Give yourself a raise. Instead of taking your annual bonus and spending on meaningless shopping sprees, you should invest in your future. Remember, a shoe collection should not be valued more than your portfolio. What brands do you love? The ones that popped into your mind are what you should research to invest. If you see that many consumers are wearing Coach and Nike, then you know that it is a great investment to begin buying shares because people are buying the products.

Financial freedom and wealth management begins with a shift in mindset. Your freedom begins with breaking loose of financial bondage and the oppression of pleasing everyone. You are capable of having everything you want if and only if you are willing to sacrifice for it.

Habit: Work toward implementing multiple streams of income, reduce debt, and create a financial plan. Schedule an appointment with a financial advisor.

****

Set Yourself Free

****

"Know that every situation brings a blessing. Find the gift, know that you have chosen to be here now and have this experience because it is helping you to grow and awaken to the glory of who you are." ~ Emma Penman

Since social media has been introduced into most households, it has become a way to share your life with people you never would have otherwise. Instead of using it as an outlet to network, it is often used as a smoking mirror. The desire to impress everyone is taking over how you personally live your life and how you feel about yourself. More people are consumed with what others think and how they live.

Bahiyah Shabazz

This thought process causes many to become trapped financially, emotionally, and psychologically. As you walk around assuming others have their lives together, many are thinking the same about you. No one realizes that each of them are still trying to figure things out.

The truth of the matter is that friends and family will only tell you what they want you to know. Some make life seem as if they have everything together and are living their dreams. When in fact their life may be a re-occurring nightmare and the only freedom they have is through the façade of what is presented.

This quickly becomes a problem because a facade leaves the impression that you are not living life to its fullest and eventually become overwhelmed with impressing

170

others instead of being content with where and who you are.

The moment you free yourself of others' expectations and make your own decisions is the moment you begin to live a wealthy lifestyle. Freedom is realizing that you have nothing else to prove.

Live on purpose

Your passion becomes your purpose. Too often, I hear about women wishing to learn what their purpose is in life. A purpose does not have to be a long, complicated act that is over the top. It is actually what you were called to do in life. A calling is drawn from the experiences you have encountered over the years. Who you are is not based on the perception of someone else. It is gained from what you have experienced.

What brings you joy?

There is always something that drives you to wake up each day with a smile on your face and ambition in your heart. Everyone is called to play a role in life. Your role is simply a piece that completes a puzzle. How many times have you spoken to someone about your goals only to have your goals shot down because no one understood why you wanted to accomplish?

Remember, your success is not for others to understand, it is for you to show the importance of what matters in your life.

Be the trailblazer for your future. No one can lead you to your destiny. They can only assist you along the way through support and accountability.

Do away with excuses

When you make excuses in life you are clearly stating that you are not worthy of what you are seeking. Too often, I hear people make plenty of excuses about why they have not completed a goal. It is either they did not have the time, resources, or money to complete them. Excuses! Excuses! Excuses! You cn make a way for what you consider is important. If you do not have a way, you create one. Do you think that successful individuals use excuses and failure as a reason to stop? Had Oprah Winfrey not been demoted from her job as a news anchor because she was not fit for television, she never would have had the Oprah Winfrey show, established the 'O Factor' and launched the Oprah Winfrey Network (OWN). Had Michael Jordan given up basketball after being cut from his high school team, he never would have been recognized as one of the best NBA players. Had Albert Einstein's parents treated him differently because he did not speak until the age of four and believed his teachers when they spoke ill of his academic performance, he never would have developed the theory of relativity.

The point is that you must not feed into the doubt of others including the doubt you have against yourself. Self-talk will either build or break your spirit. Be careful of what you think and the words you speak. One word can determine an outcome. Allow the words to build your strength. Strength is a state of mind to overcome obstacles.

A need for acceptance

A worthy life is a life of acceptance. Do not beat yourself up over mistakes. It is life's way of preparing for your destiny. As you are reading this, you are probably thinking that if I had not charged up my credit cards, taken out that loan, or learned to say no, then I would not be in the predicament I am today. It is perfectly acceptable. The decisions that you made to this point are all right.

It is not too late to accept who you have become. It is your journey to live your life on purpose through a wealthy lifestyle. You are enough!

Free yourself of the burden to please everyone while neglecting what is important to you. You have an exceptional life to live. It is time to go out and get it. A positive shift will elevate a mindset. You will notice doors will open to present opportunities. There will be an overflow of money and prayers answered.

Habit: Journal your activities each day. End the day with writing a positive message to self and how much you have developed.

****

Legacy

****

"I've learned that people will forget what you said, people will forget what you did, but people will never forget how you made them feel." ~ Maya Angelou

Who you are, what you do, how you interact with others, and make them feel becomes your legacy. Most want to be remembered in a way that will bring comfort to others while they share stories and experiences of each interaction.

While earning a Bachelor of Arts, I declared a double major. The fields were in psychology and African studies. Towards the end of the African study courses I had to record projects and write countless research papers. One of the recordings was of my grandfather who discussed his upbringing and family history. What began as a mission to earn an 'A' became an experience that will forever be remembered.

During the recording I learned how my grandfather was taught how to crop fields from his grandfather who was a slave. My grandfather only had a third grade education, which at the time was the furthest anyone had gone in the family. However, he was able to earn a living, save money, and take care of his family. As he spoke about his experiences as a child and family man, I quickly learned why he was such a miser. Living through hard times and not knowing where your next meal was coming from would do that to anyone. It was amazing to hear how his father took care of a large family by earning fifty cents a day.

At that moment, I had a new respect for my grandfather and then realized why he wanted us to earn an education and learn to take care of ourselves. He encouraged us to be independent. Jobs will come and go, friends will fade away, family may become distant and others may test you, but you will always have your education. Intelligence is the one thing that no one can ever take away from you. Education is your gift to society.

My grandfather passed away, but his words, teaching and legacy will forever live on.

What will others remember about you?

It is not too late to begin living the life that you want others to remember. Your wealth will speak for itself. It is your wealth of knowledge, your wealth of love, your wealth to help others, your wealth to share experiences, your wealth and mission of development.

Whether you believe it or not, you will leave a legacy. At this point, you have control of the type of legacy you will leave at your demise. Do not wait until it is too late, start today.

Leave a legacy of encouragement. You can use your words to lift people up or tear them down. This also begins with how you speak to yourself.

Leave a legacy of purpose. Use your strengths and talents for a purpose beyond yourself. Live a selfless life to help others and encourage having a life of continual improvement through mentoring and motivation.

Leave a legacy of excellence. Deliver and accept nothing but the best. Never allow excuses to take over your dreams and live the life that you deserve beginning with changing your habits. Your behavior will raise the standards of self and everyone who surrounds you.

Leave a legacy of love for self. You set the tone of how you wish others to treat you. In return, you encourage those who surround you to love themselves. More importantly, you learn to accept your mistakes and use as a lesson to reach your goals.

Habit: Involve yourself in a charity or nonprofit that is aligned with your goals. Take on a role that will encourage you to get out your comfort zone and to inspire others to do the same.

****

This is just the beginning

****

This is your race to win. You set the pace of how fast you want to run and the direction to take to get to the finish line. One of the best things you can do for yourself is stop comparing and listening to others. Instead, use others who are where you want to be as an *inspiration* to push forward.

Will there be obstacles? Absolutely, you will repeatedly fail. You will spend more than you earn. You will have to adjust your budget. You will give your begging cousins your last five dollars. You may even have to dissolve your company and start over. You will have to adjust your approach. Use each obstacle as a step to climb the ladder of success and have a supportive network available when you feel discouraged.

Observe your challenges and find ways to eliminate them. Successful individuals learn to incorporate positive habits into their daily routine instead of making excuses. Remember that your behavior is consistent, which means if you are disciplined, or not, in one aspect of your life your actions will continue throughout.

It would have been easy for me to discuss how to save money by using a brown bag lunch, stop drinking coffee, and save all your change. Those are methods that I am sure you have heard repeatedly. For me, wealth is more than monetary. It involves your actions. You cannot expect to be successful in your business, relationships and how you handle money, until you correct your behavior.

I am just one woman on a mission to get you to see that you are worth more than you realize. You are here for a purpose and to live the life you deserve even if that includes failing. You may not have all the money you want, but you do have the drive to get what you need. This is where it begins. Today, not tomorrow! Now let us wholeheartedly encourage activity leading to happiness and ladies do not allow anyone to convince you that it cannot be done.

My Final Thoughts

I would like to leave you with encouraging words from Marianne Williamson, author and international lecturer. Williamson says, "Our deepest fear is not that we are inadequate. Our deepest fear is that we are powerful beyond measure. It is our light, not our darkness that most frightens us. We ask ourselves, who am I to be brilliant, gorgeous, talented, fabulous? Actually, who are you *not* to be? You are a child of God. Your playing small does not serve the world. There is nothing enlightened about shrinking so that other people won't feel insecure around you. We are all meant to shine, as children do. We were born to make manifest the glory of God that is within us. It is not just in some of us; it is in everyone. And as we let our own light shine, we unconsciously give other people permission to do the same. As we are liberated from our own fear, our presence automatically liberates others."

About the author:

Bahiyah Shabazz is one of America's financial experts, economists, and TEDx Speaker. She is a business owner and occupies a position as an adjuct faculty of economics at Ivy Tech College. Shabazz has appeared in Black Enterprise, Equifax Finance, Business Insider, Rolling Out Magazine, Urban Business Roundtable, Debt.com, Black Women Expo, and various media outlets.

Learn more at www.bahiyahshabazz.com

Appendix

Data

Women and Financial Planning

- Just one-third of women have a detailed financial plan in place, and, among the youngest segment (ages 25-34), just one in 10 has a financial plan in place.
- One-quarter of women surveyed are the primary financial decision-makers in their households.
- Fewer than two in 10 women feel "very prepared" to make wise financial decisions. Half indicate that they "need some help," and one-third feels that they "need a lot of help."
- Fifty-six percent of women expect they will need to work longer and postpone retirement.
- Eighty-six percent of women do not know how to invest or choose a financial product.

Source: Financial Experience &Behaviors

among Women, 2010−2011 Prudential Research Study

In a study of women making over $30,000:

- 60% of women say they are the primary breadwinner in their households
- 12% of all women say they have not yet begun saving for retirement
- 40% of women fear ending up broke and homeless
- More than half of married women see themselves as the chief financial officer of their households
- 57% say they primarily handle major investment decisions and retirement planning themselves
- 50% of divorced women say that financial planning seems an impossible task in their lives.
- Forty-eight percent of women say that their

divorce created a financial crisis, and about two-thirds say that it made them realize the importance of financial awareness and independence.

•Over 90% of women say feel they need to be more involved in financial planning.

•62% of women expressed strong interest in learning more about finances and retirement planning

•62% of women still don't have a financial professional.

Source: Allianz Insurance 2013 Women, Money and Power Study (Insights)

Financial Statistics and Gender differences

- 50% of women find it difficult talking with others about personal finances, versus also less confident about their investment knowledge.

- Only 29% of women said they know where to invest in today's market (compared to 42% of men).

- 45% of women grade their financial literacy a 'C' or below, while 65% of men assess their level of financial literacy as a 'B' or higher. Men also express greater confidence in their ability to maintain their standard of living, with 57% feeling in good or great financial shape in this area versus 49% of women.

Source: Wells Fargo's Financial Health Study 2014

Women's Earnings

•There are 69 million women in the workforce, 10 million of them are their family's sole breadwinners.

•Women earn 77 cents for every dollar a man earns.

•Two-thirds of all working women earn less than $30,000 a year in jobs without pensions

•Women work an average of 27 years; men work an average of 40.

•Because of maternity and family leaves, which total about 13 years, retired women will receive about half the pension benefits retired men will receive.

•About 20 to 30 years are spent in retirement, and experts suggest you have at least 70 to 90 percent of your pre-retirement income saved for each retirement year to continue your current lifestyle. Women, however, need 100 percent to make up for lower pay, years out of the workforce, and longer lifespan.

•The average woman can expect to live to 80.1 years old. Men live an average of 74.8 years.

•Between ages 75 and 84, more than 60 percent of women are single or widowed. That number jumps to 87 percent after age 85.

•With the death of a spouse, women often suffer a large drop in income.

•In 2004, the median income for retired women was $12,080 compared to $21,102 for men.

•Social security replaces only about 40 percent of a worker' prior wages.

Source: What Women Need to Know about Re-
tirement: A joint project of the Heinz Family
Philanthropies and the Women's Institute for a
Secure Retirement

Women's Financial Security

- Forty-two percent of all women lack financial security
- Three out of five women over 65 cannot afford to cover their basic needs
- Only 18% of families headed by single mothers have financial security
- Marriage eases the financial burden, but most women outlive their male partners. Two-thirds of men over 65 live with a partner, while less than half (44%) of women over 65 live with a partner.
- The average annual income for an elder man ($24,300) is almost 75% higher than an elder woman's annual income ($14,000).
- The number of older women living in poverty is 50% higher than older men living in poverty.

Source: Analysis of U.S. Census data by Wider
Opportunities for Women

Women's Financial Security

- Only 7 percent of women are "very confident" in their ability to fully retire with a comfortable lifestyle.

- 43 percent of women expect to work past age 70 or do not plan to retire.

- More than half (52 percent) plan to work after they retire.

- Most (65 percent) Baby Boomer women do not have a backup plan if forced into retirement sooner than expected.

- 53 percent expect to self-fund their retirement through 401(k) or other savings and investments.

- Of women who have or plan to take time out of the workforce to be a caregiver, 74 percent believe that it will negatively impact their ability to save for retirement.

- 45 percent of women work part-time are less likely to have workplace retirement benefits.

•61 percent of women are offered a 401(k) or similar plan.

•75 percent of women who are offered an employee-funded plan participate in the plan.

•6 percent is the median contribution of women who participate in their employer's plan.

•55 percent are saving for retirement outside of work in an IRA, mutual fund, bank account, etc.

•The majority (59 percent) of women who estimate their financial need guess what their retirement savings needs would be rather than using a calculator or advisor.

•Only 35 percent of women use a professional financial advisor, most (79 percent) doing so for retirement investment recommendations.

•Many (53 percent) women want

information that is easier to understand.

Source: 14th Annual Transamerica Retirement Survey of Workers (2014)

Gender Pay Gap for 2013

•Women earned 78.3 cents for every dollar men earned in 2013, a **Census Bureau** report released [9/16/14] showed. That compares to 76.5 cents a year earlier.

Source: Wall Street Journal

Women-Owned Businesses

Numbers and Characteristics

- There are 7.8 million women-owned businesses in the United States. This reflects a 20.1% increase from 2002 to 2007.
- Women-owned firms make up 28.7% of all non-farm businesses across the country and generate $1.2 trillion in total receipts.
- A full 88.3% of these firms are non-employer firms.
- The remaining 11.7% of the firms have paid employees, employing a total of 7.6 million people across the country with a payroll of $217.6 billion. These employer firms have average receipts of $1.1 million.

Geography

- The states with the largest percentage of women-owned businesses are: District of

Columbia (34.5%), Maryland (32.6%),
New Mexico (31.7%), Hawaii (31.0%), and
Georgia (30.9%).

•The counties with the largest percentage
of women-owned businesses are: Bronx
County, NY (40.5%), Wayne County, MI
(36.7%), Kings County, NY (33.6%), and
Milwaukee County, WI (33.0%).

•The cities with the largest percentage of
women-owned businesses are: Detroit, MI
(49.7%), Baltimore, MD (36.9%),
Milwaukee, WI (36.3%), and Chicago, IL
(36.0%).

Industry

•Women-owned businesses make up more
than half (52.0%) of all businesses in health
care and social assistance.

•The other top industries for women
include: educational services (45.9% of all
businesses are women-owned),

administration and support and waste management and remediation services (37.0%), retail trade (34.4%), and arts, entertainment, and recreation (30.4%).

•Industries with the lowest percent of women-owned businesses include mining, quarrying, and oil and gas extraction (15.0%), transportation and warehousing (11.4%), agriculture, forestry, fishing, and hunting (10.3%), construction (7.9%), and management of companies and enterprises (6.7%).

Source: https://www.nwbc.gov/facts/women-owned-businesses

SOURCE: All data comes from the US Census'
2007 Survey of Business Owners. 1 Nonfarm
businesses only. Women-owned defined as a
woman or women owning 51% or more of the
company. 2 Based on the 50 most populous
counties and cities.

Notes

---

[i] http://www.whitehouse.gov/sites/default/files/rss_viewer/Women_in_America.pdf

[ii] Nces.ed.gov

[iii] Nsf.gov

[iv] Corelogic. *Corelogic.* May 1, 2012. http://www.corelogic.com/about-us/news/corelogic-reports-69,000-completed-foreclosures-nationally-in-march.aspx (accessed August 20, 2012).

[v] (Forbes)

http://www.forbes.com/sites/andreanavarro/2014/03/03/the-worlds-richest-women-2014/

[vi] Garcia, Jose. *Demos.* Nov 7, 2007. http://www.demos.org/publication/borrowing-make-ends-meet-rapid-growth-credit-card-debt-america (accessed August 28, 2012).